MW01535265

MAN CODES: **DeCODED**

A Woman's Guide to Overcoming **MAN**iPULATION

DEDICATION

This book is dedicated to every woman seeking insight and understanding. Every woman fighting to overcome.

Follow **L.J. Hamilton** on all social media platforms.

www.decodedwithlj.com

MAN CODES: **DeCODED**

A Woman's Guide to Overcoming **MANiPULATION**

Introduction – MANiPULATION Defined

Today begins your journey to overcoming! When you begin the process of detoxing and detaching from manipulative men. You've made it this far because of your strength and resilience; it's time to set yourself free from the imprisonment of manipulation. This is your new beginning!

Manipulation is defined as *managing or influencing skillfully, especially in an unfair manner; handling, managing, or using, especially with skill, in some process of treatment or performance; skillful or artful management.*[1] That's the dictionary's definition.

To better understand the direction of this book, I'll slightly tweak that definition for you.
MANiPULATION is *as a man's ability to skillfully manage or influence a woman's emotions in an unfair manner.* Manipulators love to involve themselves with

---

[1] http://dictionary.reference.com/browse/manipulation

women they can emotionally, mentally and / or physically control to ensure the success of their agenda. A lot of men have invested time in mastering their manipulative skill set to guarantee they victimize any woman they involve themselves with. The information in this book is meant to thwart that victimization. Master manipulators possess at least one of four distinct character traits that give them an unfair advantage when it comes to the women they prey on.

1. **Insight**

2. **Persuasion**

3. **Understanding**

4. **Control**

Knowing what these character traits are and how to recognize them will give you a heads up when it comes to knowing what type of man you're dealing with. Your best defense is knowledge when a master manipulator has you on his radar. He will prey on any sign of weakness. His main goal is to get you in vulnerable and compromising situations that cause you to question your better judgment. Once you let your guard down, he's going to say and do whatever it takes to get you to trust him. Afterwards, he's going to become the emotional terrorist you regret having anything to do with. He wants to break you. This makes it easier for him to manipulate you. Let's break down these character traits as they relate to **MANiPULATION** so that you'll know exactly what they look like.

1. **Insight**

   Depending on the situation, insight can be a good thing or a dangerous thing. *Insight* is a manipulative man's ability to gain an accurate and intuitive understanding of a woman.

When mastered, manipulating women is easy; choosing the right targets even easier. That's why you have to be careful when it comes to who you're vulnerable with. The wrong man will use your vulnerability against you. Oftentimes a man on a mission of manipulation will study you to gain the insight he needs. He'll actively listen and be very attentive. That's ideal right? Yes, with the right person. Not with this guy! He wants you comfortable with him. The more comfortable you are the more access you'll give. He'll want you to know that he "gets it." He'll pretend to understand what a lot of women go through when it comes to dating, relationships, societal interactions and life in general, so that he'll seem more trustworthy, like a friend. He'll use every moment of vulnerability to set you up for emotional destruction. This sounds harsh because it's supposed to. He's a predator, and predators aren't nice. He'll also reiterate that you're "safe" with him to ensure your comfort; to ensure that you open up more. Information feeds his insight, so he'll require lots of it. Being an emotional safe place for a woman all but guarantees he'll gain the insight he needs.

2. **Persuasion**

Persuasion is the action of influencing someone to do or believe something. It's a manipulative man's ability to convince you that what he's offering is in your best interest. When trying to persuade a woman to do or believe something, a manipulative man will prey on her emotionally and psychologically. He knows exactly what to say to get you thinking about something, because he knows if you're at least thinking about it there's a strong possibility that you may do or believe it. He implies a lot during conversation as a means of planting mental seeds that will hopefully work in his favor. He wants you to not only think about what he's saying, but to also feel where he's coming from. He wants you drawn in emotionally, vested in the conversation with a strong desire to do or believe exactly what he's saying or implying. During this stage of heightened emotional and mental arousal, persuading a woman to do or believe something is an almost effortless task. That's why you have to stay on guard no matter how good his words make you feel. They're just words! Protect yourself. Opening up to any man too soon is a bad idea, however opening up to a manipulative master persuader can be devastating. They're emotional terrorists, ready to cause emotional destruction. Remember that.

3. <u>**Understanding**</u>

Understanding is comprehension, and comprehension can lead to control if you're not careful. Men and women long to be understood. We want to be able to be our true selves without shame or judgment. Oftentimes we open the emotional floodgates when we feel like we've finally met someone who gets us. This is exactly what a manipulative man wants. Once you open those emotional floodgates you become easier to control. You'll begin to invest more of yourself into your involvement with him because you finally feel as though you're understood. You'll ignore the fact that he's making continual withdrawals out of your love bank without depositing anything. By the time you realize what's going on, you'll be so emotionally drained you won't have the strength to fight back against his toxicity.

Manipulative men want to understand you so they'll know what it takes to break you. They want you to reveal any brokenness so they can target you there. I'm not saying all men who understand women on some level have manipulative intentions, but you don't have time to take chances. Again, keep your guards up and protect yourself. If you feel something is off, it is. Don't trick yourself into believing otherwise. Trust your gut. Listen to your intuition. Pay attention. Never ignore red flags. A manipulative man will use his understanding of you to gain access to those parts of you kept hidden for a reason. He knows that if he can get there he can get you. He'll even open up to gain access. He'll engage in seemingly deep conversations about his emotional state to get you to expose yours, even though most if not all of what he's sharing is a lie. The more he opens up the more comfortable you feel opening up, but you have to understand that this opening up is a set up. Remember, if something feels off it is.

4. **<u>Control</u>**

When you relinquish power you give up control. When you give up control, you become a servant to the will of others. Manipulative men know this, and that's why they prey on you. They want your power, by any means necessary. They want full access. A manipulative man wants to invade your emotional space to break down any defenses you have. He wants you caught up, uncertain and sometimes afraid, because that keeps him in a position of power. He wants you so broken that you'll think no one else will want or love you. If you feel like damaged goods, what are the chances you'll want to be with anyone else? You'll start blaming yourself for his behaviors. You'll find yourself doing what he tells you just to keep the peace; walking on eggshells hoping that you don't set him off to the point of verbally and / or physically abusing you. The emotional and mental abuse you will force yourself to endure will become a heavier burden to bear the longer you stay. You'll become lost in him, questioning yourself as to why you're remaining in such a toxic situation. You'll convince yourself that if you could just do this or that, maybe he'll change. You'll make plans to leave, but never follow though. Understand, there's absolutely nothing you can do to make him change. He is who he is. He has to decide to change for himself. You're putting his needs before yours, and the longer this toxic relationship continues the more of yourself you'll lose. He's controlling every aspect of the relationship. He doesn't want you to have a say, he just wants you to listen. He's a narcissist. An abuser. He knows that as long as you allow him to control you, you'll never leave. That's his greatest fear. You leaving and staying gone. This type of man needs a woman to control or he feels inadequate.

Breaking Free

My goal is to help you learn how to recognize the signs of a manipulative man, and unlearn certain behaviors that make you easy prey. The four character traits will be revisited as you read. You will gain more insight as to how to deal with and detach from manipulative men. You will learn what red flags to look for and what to do when you feel hopeless. I hope to empower you and to inspire growth and change in your life. There are a lot of manipulative men out there; I want to help you navigate your way through and away from them. I have been that manipulative man. I mastered the game and used it to hurt women because I was hurt.

I treated women unkindly because I felt love had been unkind to me. I blamed them for my pain. While I've never physically abused a woman, my toxic behaviors were just as bad, if not worse. I know what I'm talking about. I mastered manipulation from a young age. Starting with my mother and into adulthood, manipulating almost every woman who was unfortunate enough to find herself involved with me. That's not something I'm proud of. With this book I hope to experience some measure of redemption. I hurt women on purpose. I caused them extreme amounts of sadness and emotional suffering. I still carry the shame of these behaviors with me, and that's why I feel an obligation to help women understand about men what a lot women didn't understand about me. This book is a freeing experience for you and for myself. This isn't a man-hating book. This is a book that will help you avoid men who actually hate women. Men who use and abuse women. Men who manipulate women. This book is about to change your life.

Trust me. I want you to be able to recognize manipulation when you feel and see it. Master manipulators have studied women. Now it's your turn to study them. They've had the advantage, but this book is a game changer. Manipulative men aren't hard to recognize once you have the blueprint. This book is the blueprint. Be ready to put in the work. It doesn't matter how many self-help books you read if you don't apply the knowledge you receive. Don't invest the time if you're not willing to do the work. Be ready to take what you learn and apply it to your daily life, breaking bad dating and relationship habits in the process.

Chapter One – The Most Dangerous **MAN**iPULATORS

Master manipulators usually go undetected. In most cases they're not recognized until it's too late. In this chapter I will highlight the more covert signs you need to be aware of so you'll know which types of men to stay away from. Knowing exactly what to look for and expect is imperative to successful dating and relationship navigation. Without guidance you can easily end up lost in a sea of toxic masculinity and manipulation. I don't want that for you. The following four men are the most dangerous manipulators. Have a pen and paper handy because I'm going to give you some tips on how to recognize, avoid and / or detach from these types of men. Take notes.

<u>Manipulator One</u> – The "Sensitive" Manipulator

The most dangerous type. He uses sensitivity and attentiveness to reel you in. He comes across as "different" from other guys. You feel an almost immediate connection, but why? Was it something he said? Something he did? Do you even know? He's the type to prey on your emotions, so vulnerability is a must. He'll want to talk a lot about you and how you feel about anything, but about men, dating and relationships especially. He'll dig, he'll pry, but not in a way that seems intrusive and makes you uncomfortable, but in a way that causes you to think he's genuinely interested. He wants you to let your guard down. He wants full access. He wants you to expose any weakness you have, because in doing so you become an easier target to manipulate. He's an emotional predator who specializes in covert operations for the sole purpose of planting explosives that will ruin your life when detonated. He wants you to hurt. He wants you broken. He's hurt and broken but reusing to admit and deal with his issues. He wants you to suffer like he's suffering so he'll do whatever it takes to cause you heartache once given full access. He wants to take his misery out on you, on purpose. It's not right. It's not fair. It's a harsh reality. Because he lacks compassion, he can use what appears to be sensitivity without actually being sensitive. In the beginning he can cause you to feel amazing, even though his goal is to hurt you. Most "sensitive" manipulators are narcissists or have narcissistic tendencies that add severity to the damage they are capable of causing.

Combating the "Sensitive" Manipulator

This is war! Emotional combat! You must save yourself! It's time to arm yourself with the weaponry needed to ensure emotional survival and well-being. It must be understood that every seemingly nice guy isn't a nice guy, and you may be the target of his emotional terrorism. You can't let your guards down and relinquish your power just because he makes you feel good. Feeling good wears off quick when you know what signs to look for. Pay close attention to what's being said and what's being done to make you feel "good", and ask yourself why. Directly question him on his motives, because all men have them. You'll be able to tell if he's being honest or not. Ask yourself why he's digging, prying and being overly inquisitive? Is it really about you, or is it about his plans for you? Is it really about getting to know you, or is it about positioning you for manipulation? Trust your gut. It'll tell you everything you need to know. Not all sensitive guys are manipulators but a lot of them are, and they use being "sensitive" to cause emotional destruction. Men like this are harboring pain, but their pain isn't your problem, and you have to make sure you're not victimized because of it. He'll break your heart and move on to the next woman like you never existed. That's how little you mean to him. That's why you have to be careful when a man seems too good to be true. In most cases he is, and you're being set up for a major letdown.

You Don't Have to Be a Victim!

Be careful not to expose yourself or any weaknesses to the wrong man. Keep all areas of vulnerability private until you get a clear look at his game plan. Every man haa one; every man has an agenda. Don't give access too soon. Make a man earn it, and afterwards make sure he deserves it before you give it. Even the nicest guys don't deserve that type of clearance unless you know for certain they're worth investing in and receiving investments from. If you feel he's worth it, take the time to feel him out before you let him in. If he feels you're worth it he won't mind you practicing patience; he'll actually understand and encourage it. Keep him at an emotionally safe distance until you know that it's safe to be vulnerable. Trust your instincts. Growth takes time. Don't let him rush you, even if he's saying and doing all the right things. You're not going to miss out on anyone or anything of value just because you decide to do what's best for you. Keep your eyes open and never ignore red flags; you're being warned about something for a reason. Time is the best defense you have when it comes to dealing with "sensitive" manipulators. They hate investing more time than they feel is required to begin causing damage. Eventually their true colors will show, and you'll be glad you kept an emotionally safe distance when they do. Time is on your side, and it's the one thing that makes him most uncomfortable when it comes to manipulating women. He knows it's out of his control. He hates that! If he's not worth the time or effort, move on. If you want to see how things progress, be careful and pay attention.

Manipulator Two – The Verbal Manipulator

I'm sure you've heard the old saying "talk is cheap."
There is no better example of that than the verbal
manipulator. Yes he has game, but that's about it. If
given the opportunity, he'll effortlessly talk you into
or out of something without you catching on to the
fact that he's setting you up for manipulation. If he
can't talk his way into it he won't do it. It may sound
good to you, but is it good for you? He'll talk you
out of everything from your clothes to your credit
card if you don't tune him completely out, because
his main goal is to get as much as he can as quickly
as possible. He can't stick around long because he
knows you'll eventually get hip to the lies and
broken promises. He knows you'll begin to have
expectations that he can't fulfill. He's a consummate
verbal manipulator who will say whatever it takes to
get whatever he wants. He'll make you laugh a lot,
because he knows that's one of the best ways to help
a woman feel comfortable . He'll ask specific

questions but in a non-invasive manner, just to gauge where you are emotionally and mentally. Different levels of emotional and mental maturity require different tactics of manipulation. He's a talker; he wants you to know that he knows how to communicate. It's his primary skillset, so expect hm to be very good with words.

Combating the Verbal Manipulator

How much of your time are you willing to waste and emotional well-being are you willing to sacrifice over words that carry no real significance? His words can definitely be misleading if you let him draw you in with his rhetoric and embellishments? This is when you take control of the conversation. Don't let him persuade you to play you. He's good with game, but you know game when you hear it. You may even call him on it. He'll deny that it's game with one of those "This is just me. This is the way I talk" responses, but you know BS when you hear it. When the alarm goes off in your head, stop him in his tracks. Nothing more needs to be said. You're being forewarned for a reason; he's dangerous! He's not right, and you can feel that. Don't ignore that feeling and don't let him talk you out of feeling it.

You Don't Have to Be a Victim!

You're not obligated to continue conversing with him. Once you get that forewarning, cut everything else off! You're getting bad vibes for a reason, even if he looks and sounds like the perfect gentleman. Don't give him the benefit of the doubt and set yourself up for heartache. The vibe outweighs the words, and the energy is trying to redirect you; let it. He's trying to verbally manipulate you. Don't let it happen! If you choose to continue the conversation, do so understanding that your emotional and mental well-being is your territory, and you have an obligation to protect it. He'll use his words to infiltrate your territory, and that's why keeping your guards up is crucial. You control the direction and flow of the conversation until you feel comfortable loosening the reins. That's if you really want to take that chance. Understand, you're rolling the dice and things might not work out in your favor. If you're a woman who likes to give a man a chance, make sure you remain in control when you do. These are delicate areas of your life that you don't want damaged again. You have every right to keep yourself at an emotionally safe distance until you choose otherwise. That's your decision, not his. Don't let him talk you into giving him the power to make the decision for you.

Manipulator Three – The Space Invader

The space invader needs physical contact in order for him to make his move. The closer he gets to you the easier it'll be for him to manipulate the situation. He wants to be in your space sexually and / or physically (in your home) so he can use his presence to manipulate your behaviors and responses. He'll test boundaries to see how far you'll let him go, and how far you're willing to go. He's a man who generally has problems verbally expressing his need for attention, and while wanting someone's attention isn't a bad thing, when the actions aren't reciprocated and beneficial for both parties someone is going to be left hanging. He's a narcissist, like most manipulators. He wants to be in your space, placing demands on your time and body that he has no right to place. He needs attention, sex and other physical acts of service in order to feel like he's serving his purpose in your life. He needs to dominate you. Like most manipulators, there's an emotional black hole inside of him that makes him devoid of compassion and concern. How you feel about what he's doing to you doesn't matter. He'll constantly seek physical gratification until you figure out what he's really doing. That's when he'll stage a disappearing act. He wants you to forgo rational thought during initial interactions. He wants to infect your common sense in hopes that you won't use it when dealing with him. He'll do everything in his power to increase sexual tension; that's why it's so important for him to be in your space. Making you want him is key because in his mind it excuses him from any blame or accountability when things go sideways. He wants a sexual and physical relationship with you. Nothing more. He wants to have sex with you. He wants to live / be in your home minus actually contributing anything to it. He wants you to be his 2 a.m. booty call. He wants your bed to be the bed he can find rest in if he doesn't have a place of his own. He wants you to become the woman you swore you'd never be so he can reap the benefits of that bad decision.

Combating the Space Invader

The space invader is good at what he does, and he's used to women giving in. It's up to you to set boundaries and enforce limitations. Should he be that close to you? Should he be touching you that way? Has he earned time and / or free reign in your home, especially without contributing to it? He's pressing you and pressuring you, even though he's being discreet about it. Think about why. He wants what you have, and doesn't want to give up anything to get it.

You Don't Have to Be a Victim!

You have the power to determine your level of sexual and physical interaction with this man, if any. I recommend getting away from this man! He doesn't hide his intentions well because closeness and physical touch is a must in order for him to be successful, so you'll be able to quickly tell what he's on by what he does. Even when attraction is strong you have to be on guard, especially when he becomes covertly inappropriate, because there's a reason he's trying to make you feel a certain type of way as quickly as he can. A skilled space invader will target specific generally more sensitive areas on your body; ears, lips, neck, breast area, knee, thigh, or waist. He'll attempt to touch you in those places in a non-intrusive manner, hoping the contact leads to arousal. Stop him if this isn't what you want! You are in control of your space, so control who you let into it. Don't feel guilty about telling him to stop, and take this red flag to mean it's time to shut down his game plan. Men like this will say and do anything to invade your space. Unless there's a mutual understanding, never give any man that kind of power or control over your body!

<u>**Manipulator Four**</u> – The Needy Manipulator

The needy manipulator is just that – NEEDY! He preys on vulnerable women who feel some form of validation when doing for their man. This doesn't make them bad, but it does make them more susceptible to the needy manipulator's advances.

Most women who find themselves caught up with taking care of a needy manipulator are women who have a desire to feel needed. When that care and concern isn't reciprocated, eventually these women begin to feel emotionally drained, unsatisfied and stressed. This is when they realize they're more of a caretaker than an actual partner. A needy manipulator will guilt trip the you know what out of a woman when she refuses to do something he asks (or tells) her to do. He's like a child who has a constant need for something, and he wants you to feel like it's your responsibility to serve and please him. He wants you to be his "other mother" and to feel obligated to make sure he's taken care of. He refuses to outgrow this childlike mentality because with that comes adult accountability and responsibility. The needy manipulator is the man who refuses to work, yet always asks you for money. The man who will convince you that it's a financially intelligent decision for him to move in with you. The man who will have you purchase a cell phone for him in your name, drive your car, expect you to fill up the tank, and then get upset with you for not doing so. As hard to believe as it may be, there are definitely men like this just waiting for women to come along and take care of them. I am an advocate for relationships that find each person doing equally for the other, and if one happens to fall on hard times I also believe the other person should be there for encouragement and support. However, needy manipulators exist in hard times, or stay in some form of drama that they need to be rescued from; they always expect their significant other to do the rescuing. If there is no reciprocation of care, provision and support, then you're nothing more than a caretaker. Needy manipulators are opportunists who prey on vulnerable women, seeking maximum benefits in exchange for minimal effort.

Combating the Needy Manipulator

You have to pay extra close attention when dealing with a suspected needy manipulator because their actions are gradual and may take some time. They will test limitations by asking for things on a smaller scale or by making seemingly innocent demands to see what they can get away with and get out you. The goal is how much. How much can I get out of you in exchange for nothing? If you're not careful, you'll find yourself caught up and possibly in love with a man who is more like your son, thus making it even harder to disconnect from him. This can also be considered a form of psychological manipulation, especially if you desire a son or have become estranged from or lost one.

You Don't Have to Be a Victim!

If the relationship is still in its beginning stages, certain requests should be clear signs that he's a needy manipulator. If he expects you to pay for all the dates, you need to be careful. If he doesn't have the essentials a typical adult would need to live comfortably (i.e., employment, a running vehicle, a place to live other than a parent's basement, etc.), you need to be careful. If you find yourself driving him everywhere he needs and wants to go, paying any type of bill(s) for him, or loaning him money regularly, you need to be careful. We fall on hard times. I get it. But instead of getting comfortable in cyclical patterns of hard times, we should do whatever it takes to escape and avoid them. Even still, through those hard times we should evolve, grow and improve, and not expect anyone to take care of us because we refuse to do the work. Distinction is key. The best way to combat a needy manipulator is to set clear limitations and expectations and say no when you feel enough is enough. This is not mean, this is protective. It's your responsibility to keep yourself safe from every type of manipulator and emotional terrorist. Now you know what signs to look for. Stand firm on not becoming a needy manipulator's caretaker. Any man who can't take care of himself shouldn't involve himself with a woman and expect her to. If he can't do for himself, what can he do for you? Outside of dire circumstances, if the care, concern, support and provision isn't being reciprocated, perhaps the two of you don't need to be together. Various types of manipulators exist. These four are the most dangerous. No woman deserves the kind of pain these men cause, yet it happens every day. Millions of men get away with manipulating women because the signs aren't always as clear as they should be. Hopefully this information illuminates some things for you.

Chapter Two – So What's the Difference?

Because of their experiences, a lot of women are convinced that all men are the same. While this may be true in a sense, there are some distinct characteristics that separate the good from the bad. Most men share common personality traits. Certain behaviors, coping mechanisms and problem solving skills can be attributed to most men, however when dealing with manipulators you have to take notice of the behaviors that put them in a separate category. I will highlight three types of men and the differences between each to help you separate the good from the bad.

Imposters, Impressers & Investors

Imposters

Imposters are posers. Men who want you to think they're someone and something they're not. They try hard to be the perfect guy because they want to give you this inflated perception of them to make manipulating you easier. They seem too good to be true but they're actually covert emotional terrorists. They say all the right things and make all the right moves because they're experts at manipulating women. Their only concern is what they can get out of you. Their ego and narcissism desensitizes them to the pain they cause, and they've mastered being deceptive and dishonest. They're leeches who feed off of information; the more you give the better you position them to manipulate you. They'll even pretend to open up but that's only to make you feel more comfortable with being vulnerable. They're the demanding take charge type who don't take kindly to being told no. They want what they want, and if you're a means to an end they'll use you to get there. Again, beware of a man digging for lots of personal information without waiting until you're comfortable enough to naturally share certain things with him. His heightened sense of urgency is a set up. You don't owe that level of access to someone you just met. Don't let him rush you into revealing too much too soon. Take your time. Remain in control of the interaction and conversation. If you sense he's up to no good, more than likely he is and that's your cue to cut off all contact. There's nothing genuine about him, and the quicker you realize this the better.

Impressers

Impressers are all about using status, position and possessions to hook you. They want you to want them because of who they are and what they have, so they can use those things to string you along during what will definitely be an emotionally turbulent involvement. They seek women who look the part, who would represent them well but not outshine them. More often than not they're very polished, so they want you to be polished as well – at all times. They'll definitely complain when you're not. They've mastered talking the talk, and when in social settings they will present (not introduce) you to others as if they were showing off their latest acquisition. You're an object to them, nothing more. Once you serve your purpose you'll no longer be of any use. Impressers feel great accumulations of wealth, power, status and material things guarantee successful interactions with women because they think most women would rather have material things than love. They fear being taken advantage of so, out of everything they show, very little is shared. Beware of a man who speaks way too highly of himself and his accomplishments; a man who makes extravagant decrees and promises without knowing the type of woman you are. He's setting you up to be manipulated. He's the man who will offer you the comforts of his beautiful home but kick you out of it when he's done with you. He's the man who will give you the keys to his luxury car but leave you on the side of the road if you say or do something he doesn't like. Yes this happens, a lot. Don't be blinded by his charm or charisma; neither proves that he's a good guy. If you look the part, he wants you for one purpose: To show off until it's time to upgrade. Is that a harsh thing to say? Of course, but it's the truth. Impressers aren't nice, so I can't be nice when detailing their intentions. To them women are possessions, and every possession has an expiration date. In their eyes, your shelf life is from when you first meet to when they meet someone they think looks the part better than you.

Investors

Investors are about getting to know you and actually building something with you over time. Relationships are important to them and they understand the work involved in ensuring things flow smoothly. This is why they seek a legitimate connection with a woman they see themselves with long-term; they're ready for commitment. They want a life partner, a return on their investment that usually includes love, marriage and family. They want to know where you stand on all of that so expect them to be very inquisitive and observant. He wants a relationship where each person makes the other better. Generally speaking, investors are secure in themselves and stable in their lives. They've invested time in personal and emotional growth and development, so meeting the right woman is key. They don't like to date around; they're looking to settle down. Foundational understanding is important, so expect conversations about where you see yourself in the near and distant future. In most cases they want a wife. Quality time together is a must, and they easily develop an admiration for the woman they can see themselves committing to. They're understanding because they actually take the time to listen to understand. You'll get to the point where you're comfortable enough to be open, honest, transparent and vulnerable with them without fear of being shamed, targeted or judged. Manipulators are all about getting what they want from women and hurting them. An investor may find that he has to be a man of action to help restore a woman's faith and trust in men, even though he didn't cause any of the damage. If he feels she's worth the investment, he'll make it.

Winners & Spinners

As you learn the difference between various types of men, it's also important to be able to recognize winners and spinners. By now I'm sure you understand that manipulating men are very strategic, they have a game plan when it comes to you, so your methods of combat have to be just as strategic.

Winners

Winners have a lot of the attractive qualities that most women look for in a man. The following winning characteristics are a few that you need to be mindful of when dating and developing relationships:

- > **Time** – When a man understands that patience is key, that's a man you may want to take a closer look at.

- > **Confidence** – I've never met a woman who wanted a man who lacked confidence. It shouldn't cause him to be arrogant or pushy, but confidence should cause him to stand out.

- > **Responsive** – It's very important that you involve yourself with a man who doesn't fear communicating openly. You never want to do all the talking, and you never want to be on the receiving end of a conversation all about him. He should listen just as well as he responds, and conversing with him shouldn't make you feel uncomfortable.

- > **Giving** – Everything he requires he's willing to give. That's how partnerships work.

These are just a few of the winning characteristics you should be mindful of as you look to involve yourself with someone; more will be detailed as you read further. Although there will be other characteristics about him that you (specifically) will find attractive, never lose sight of the fact that you want a man who contributes to your happiness, makes you feel amazing and helps you grow.

Spinners

Spinners, as I like to call them, spin every phase of the relationship to ensure it benefits them. The following spinning characteristics are a few that you need to be mindful of when dating and developing relationships:

> **Selfishness** – They care more about self-preservation than partnership.

➢ **Insensitive** – Their wants and needs is their focus; what you want and need doesn't matter. They'll try to make you feel less than, hoping that you realize that pleasing them is more important than anything that involves you and your happiness.

Leeches – Spinners will latch on to you and drain your time, energy, and sometimes self-worth if they can. They want you to expose areas of brokenness to one day use against you.

Winners seek purpose, while spinners seek posture. One definition for *purpose* is *an intended or desired result; end; aim; goal.*[2] Winners have an intended or desired result in mind when they invest in you. They have a plan that centers around partnership.

---

[2] http://dictionary.reference.com/browse/purpose

Posture means *to position, esp. strategically, and to act in an affected or artificial manner, as to create a certain impression.*[3] Spinners seek posture. They're like crooked politicians who will say and do anything to gain ground and win elections. Spinners are strategic and their agenda is their focus. You don't matter. Not for real anyway. You're feelings aren't important. What they have to say sounds good but you have to be smarter and well-prepared in order to beat them at their game. Don't fall for the spin because it'll make you too dizzy to pay attention to what's really going on. In general, most men share common character traits and behavioral patterns, but many are different when it comes to intention. What are they really in it for? I can't definitively say what a "real man" is because it's subjective based on personal views, opinions and feelings. I can say what a real man isn't. A real man isn't one who has ill intentions when it comes to the women he involves himself with. A real man isn't dishonest or deceitful. Most men would

---

[3] http://dictionary.reference.com/browse/posture

agree, we're not that complex but we can be tricky if women don't take the time to read us correctly. If only all of these dating and relationship dynamics were simple right? If only we were born knowing who our soul-mates were and where to find them. Unfortunately, many of us have never found and may never find the one who fits us perfectly. We'll continue going through life entangled in unhealthy relationship after unhealthy relationship; we'll continue trying to change unchangeable people. Ladies, it only takes one moment to meet the man who will impact your life the most, whether that's in a positive or negative way. If you feel he's worth it, take the time to discover who he really is and then make an informed decision to stay or go. Don't invest feelings too fast and don't ever make decisions based on the belief that you can change him. Be present, in the moment. If he's not who you want right now, he won't be who you want after you waste five years trying to change him. You deserve better. You know it and I know it. How many more abusive relationships will you suffer through before you see and appreciate your value and understand that you're better than that and deserve better than him? In many ways all men are *"just alike"*, but it's up to you to determine who to open the floodgates of your heart to. It's up to you to make informed relationship decisions and not decisions based on impulse, neediness or vulnerability. Keep your guards up and read on. We're just getting started.

Chapter Three – Stop Setting Yourself Up to be Hurt

In order for hurt to be dealt with properly it has to be acknowledged and accepted. It can't be ignored or suppressed. It won't just go away on its own. The hut has to be seen for what it is and why it is instead of being left where it is. Until you heal, your brokenness will always attract predators. Wounded prey is the easiest to devour, and when a manipulator senses or becomes aware of your pain, he'll attack you there.

The Hurt Caused by Others

It's self-explanatory really, so we won't spend a lot of time on it. This is when someone close to you hurts you, or someone who may not be all that close but has enough access to do damage. All of us have been hurt by someone we love(d) and / or care(d) about. It can definitely be a disappointing and trying experience. Because we love and because we care, we can't and don't just get over it. If we never deal with it, it will eventually infect us emotionally the longer we pretend it's not there. Hurt always matters. It's important to acknowledge its presence, its power and its hold. Once you do that, the healing process can begin.

Self-Imposed Hurt

This happens when red flags are ignored. When you know the right thing to do, but you give a person the benefit of the doubt instead. When what they want is more important than what you need, which is to get as far away from them as possible. This is you, allowing yourself to be hurt. Opening yourself up to be hurt. Becoming so used to pain that the absence of it causes you to question if it's wrong to be involved without its presence. This is the hurt that really breaks you, emotionally and mentally, because you blame yourself more than you do the person who hurt you. You tear yourself down because you knew you should've never been involved or stay involved, but you did despite your better judgement. You brought this hurt on yourself, and while it's not your fault that they hurt you, you must be willing to acknowledge and accept your role in the pain they caused in order to experience total and complete healing.

The Set-Up. Acceptance. Moving Forward

Have you ever been involved with a man who you knew couldn't love you the right way? Who didn't know how to treat you? How to please you emotionally, mentally and intimately? A man who completely ignored your love languages and any other relationship needs you had? Instead of leaving him did you find yourself trying to change him? Stranded in a headed nowhere fast relationship hoping to wake up to someone different? Missing out on everything you desire and the type of love you deserve because you kept clinging to potential and possibility? How many times have you done this, and how many years have you wasted doing it?? This is what I call the set-up. Believe it or not, you set yourself up for failure every time you've done this; every time you do this. There's a 99% chance that things won't work in your favor. Why would a man change if he knows you accept him the way he is? You may not like it but you accept it, and he knows this. Why would a man change if he sees no value in changing or in you? Never (again) fall for the *"Just be patient with me, and I'll change. I just need your help."* Nonsense! This excuse is just another form of manipulation. If he had any real interest in changing he would've done it long before you. He knows he's toxic. He won't change until he's ready, if ever! His change isn't dependent on you or your presence in his life, and he'll always be who he is as long as women continue to accept his behaviors and make excuses for him being that way. Don't let the *what if* syndrome keep you chained to an unhealthy relationship. *"What if he changes and we're not together?"* Honestly, that shouldn't be your concern. It's time to put yourself first! You won't miss out. Trust me. *"What if he really needs me in order to change?"* He doesn't. You've been manipulated to the point of no longer focusing on your needs or overall well- being. Now it's about him and what he might do, even though chances are he won't. Ask the *what ifs* this way: *What if he never changes? What if he ends up breaking your heart and hurting? What if he gets and starts treating you worse?* Then what? If you're going to have questions, at least set them up to be fair to yourself. You're setting yourself up for failure when you think you can change a man. No woman has the power to do that. His change is on him. Can you influence some measure of change in his life? Maybe. But he still has the power to accept or deny that influence. You already know the relationship is headed nowhere, so why stay? You have this false sense of hope that change is on the way. It's not, and it's time to let him go and focus on you and your healing.

Break the pattern! Stop crying over men who never deserved you. Give up on men who gave up on you a long time ago. Stop using your hurt as a crutch, allowing your pain to make you an easy target for more hurt. Just like his change is on him, your healing is on you. It's time to stop blaming yourself. Accept what happened and prepare to move forward. Don't become or remain a woman scorned. Pursue healing, experience healing, and celebrate your growth through the process of healing. Once you get to this point what once made you an easy target for manipulation will no longer exist because those predator attracting wounds will heal, and the memories of those who caused them will be replaced with a new found freedom. Don't continue setting yourself up. You're better than that. Make the hard decision to look at yourself and acknowledge your role in your pain, then set it in your mind that you'll never again be a victim! His toxicity is not your fault, but you owe it to yourself to never again have the same lapse in judgment, give the same benefit of the doubt, or waste more time on men you know are no good for you. Levels exist for a reason. They're not on your level. You know it. They know it. So act like it! Accountability is always a hard pill to swallow, but self-accountability is a vital step in the healing process. Take the focus off of him and put it on yourself. He may never apologize for what he did to you, and that's okay. Forgive yourself for what you allowed to happen. Yes you are the victim, and never would I blame the victim for their victimization, but you have to do all that you can to ensure you won't be victimized again; that includes making better choices when it comes to men. Focus on any areas where you feel change is needed in your life, focus on your emotional and mental well-being, and take the time to heal. Don't rush the process. Deal with the damage and allow time for repair. Remember, a man who genuinely loves you will never manipulate you. Granted even the best men make mistakes, but it's the manipulating ones that cause the most pain. As you gain this understanding of manipulative men, also understand that you don't have to be a victim any longer! Stop giving the benefit of the doubt to men who don't deserve it, stop giving yourself to men who don't deserve you, and always choose you. No matter what, always choose you.

Chapter Four – Why You Keep Attracting the Same Types of Men

When it comes to dating and relationships are you beginning to notice a pattern? You keep attracting the same types of men and that's the reasons things aren't working out successfully. Believe it or not you're attracting the types of men you want to be involved with. The types you give the most energy to in thought, action and speech. I know it sounds crazy, but let me explain. *Attraction* means *the act, power, or property of attracting; attractive quality; magnetic charm; fascination; allurement; enticement; a characteristic or quality that provides pleasure; attractive feature.*[4] What types of men are drawn to you most of the time? I'm willing to bet you know someone who has great opportunities knocking at their door all the time? You could be that person. This happens because they're attracting those opportunities. They're giving life to them in thought, action and speech. They're

---

[4] http://dictionary.reference.com/browse/attraction

manifesting positive outcomes no matter what. They have bad moments but their entire day isn't defined by them. They're always looking for the silver lining instead of wallowing under the dark cloud. In return, good things are attracted to them. It's karma. What you give out comes back. This works in every area of life, including dating and relationships. Law of attraction isn't easily quantified, yet it has certain characteristics associated with it that may help understand why you're attracting the same types of man.

Law of Attraction

"The phrase "law of attraction," though used widely by esoteric writers, does not have a consensual definition. However, the consensus among thinkers, such as William Walker Atkinson and Sri K. Parvathi, part of the New Thought movement, is that the law of attraction is based on the principal "like attracts like" and applies it to conscious desire. Both are among many credible New Thought thinkers

who published successful books and articles related to the law of attraction. The basis of the theory (or "law") is that a person's thoughts (conscious and subconscious), emotions, and beliefs cause a change in the physical world that attracts positive or negative experiences or people that correspond to the aforementioned thoughts; with or without the person taking action to attain such experiences. This process has been described as "harmonious vibrations of the law of attraction," or "you get what you think about; your thoughts determine your experience." The initial phrase is closely associated with New Thought beliefs and practices, from which its most common definition arises, but it also has a longstanding (and more complex development) in other fields such as Hermeticism and Theosophy." [5] According to the concept of *"like attracts like"*, who and / or what you think about most is what's attracted to you most often. Think about the men you attract most of the time. Am I wrong? You've met men you were attracted to and men you weren't attracted to. You gave the men

---

[5] Source for documented Law of Attraction and New Thought thinkers information- www.jedi.wikia.com/wiki/Law_of_Attraction

you were attracted to your attention. The others you didn't. You felt a vibe. You felt chemistry. You liked them. And there's nothing wrong with any of that, but always be open to questioning why them, especially when things don't work out. Where did that attraction, vibe and chemistry go? Was it ever really there? Believe it or not, you can control what kind of men you attract and are attracted to. You should quickly be able to tell if things are real or imitations. Things that lead you to believe something is when it really isn't. Let's look at five reasons you may be attracting the same types of men and what can be done to shift things in your favor.

1. **What You Think About Most**

What you think about most is what's drawn to you most often. This is how the universe responds to your thoughts. Law of attraction doesn't judge what you're thinking, it only responds by giving it to you within reason. Of course you can't just think about 1 million dollars and have it fall out of the sky for you. However you can deliberately create what you want in your life by choosing what you think about most. You can literally manifest good or bad based on mentality; yes these rules apply when it comes to men. As long as you give more thought to negative men, you're going to keep attracting them. That energy will keep you on their radar. It may sound weird but mastering this simple concept is life-changing. Law of attraction is always reflecting what you're thinking about most and projecting into the atmosphere. That's how bad moments become bad days. You spend all day thinking about that one bad moment, and in turn that causes your entire day to be bad. You can start manifesting the life you want by applying the following:

Ask – Think about, identify and then ask for the type of men you want attracted to you. Ask who? Yourself! Who knows you and the desires of your heart better than you?

Answer – Your answer(s) come according to your thoughts and what they project into the atmosphere. Changing the way you think changes the answers you receive.

Receive – Be open to new types of men and experiences that will begin to be attracted to you. Don't ask for answers, receive them and then reject them because they're unfamiliar. Changing the way that you think changes the universal law of attraction and the type of men you're attracting.

2. <u>A Shift Doesn't Exist</u>

When you never step outside of your routine or your box, what do you expect to happen? A familiar environment is not always good when it comes to a happier more fulfilling dating life. Never doing anything different will leave you stuck in a dating rut, attracting jerk after jerk after jerk. It's time to venture outside of your comfort zone; to change your environment and discover new places to go and new things to do. Expanding your circle of friends is also helpful. You never know who someone knows or who you may encounter while hanging out with new people. Don't miss out the possibility because you refuse to shake things up a bit. When you do something different you may attract someone different. When you open yourself up to new experiences you may experience someone new in the process.

3. <u>Expecting Something for Nothing</u>

There's nothing wrong with weekends spent snuggled up in your bed or on your sofa with some vanilla bean ice cream and endless hours of Lifetime movies. It lacks romantic spark, but there's nothing wrong with it. However if this routine is keeping you from meeting new people, you need to turn the television off and turn your social life on. Is social media your most reliable source for meeting new men? If so, you need to put down your mobile device and make it a point to experience life outside of virtual reality. You can't expect something magical to happen when your efforts are minimal at best. If your heart's desire is to meet the man of your dreams, you can't put little effort into making that happen. You can't spend all of your free time secluded, watching Prince Charming romance the broken-hearted damsel in the movie, hoping that the same thing will happen for you. It won't. Not at the rate you're going. One reason you aren't meeting "Mr. Right" could be your expectation for him to just appear without you having to do any real work to cross paths with him. He's not going to just show up at your door on bended knee asking for your hand in marriage. Meeting different types of men, dating and potentially developing a healthy relationship takes you investing time and effort into making the magic happen. Every guy you meet will not be a winner but you never know when you'll cross paths with the future love of your life. In order for that to happen he has to be able to see and meet you. Put more effort into the serendipity of it all. Even if it takes going out to the movies or to dinner by yourself (this isn't a sad or bad thing), do something to show yourself available and interested in the right man. Prince Charming doesn't know you're out there if you're not out there.

4. <u>Eliminating Options and Possibilities (Sometimes Unknowingly)</u>

Your list of must haves may actually be putting a damper on your dating and love life. Pause for a minute and think about it. Granted all of us have standards and expectations that we'd like our future partner(s) to meet, but when there's no exceptions to the rules we make it harder to be open to other types of individuals, personalities and experiences that may actually be better for us. Expectations like stability, good listening and communication skills, and trustworthiness should never be compromised. Others like matching incomes, height requirements and social status would be more beneficial to you if tweaked a bit or eliminated altogether. You're attracted to what you're attracted to, I get it, but you'll miss out on the man of your dreams because he's only 5'10" and you refuse to date anyone under 6'. Believe it or not, a lot of women place huge emphasis on things that count for nothing when matters of the heart are being examined. His car and money can do nothing for you when you're questioning your relationship. Sometimes the must have list is the biggest factor as to why you're still single or unhappily involved with someone looks good on paper. You'll never experience true love unless your standards are practical, meaningful and attainable. Of course attraction is important, and I'm not saying give your number and / or spend time with every man you meet. I'm saying be open to other options and possibilities. Sometimes Mr. Right won't be determined by check marks.

He may be the guy you're overlooking because of them.

5. <u>Fear Factors and Obstacles</u>

After heartache you can and should expect to experience some level of fear when it comes to dating and relationships; at least for a while. You don't want to be hurt again so you'll become guarded and have reservations when it comes to granting access to someone new. Failed relationship after relationship will leave you feeling like true love isn't in the cards for you and remaining single is best, even though that's not what you really want. A manipulative man can sense that fear. He can pinpoint your reservations and attack you where you're weakest. Manipulative men know how to get around the hurdles you set in place to detour them. They're experts at it. That's why you keep attracting them unknowingly. They're drawn to hurt and fearful women like sharks are to blood in water. They prowl ready to attack and devour you, and sometimes you don't have the strength to fight them off; your pain has zapped you of it. Your pain is the obstacle you need to get over in order to ward off manipulators and position yourself for dating and relationship success. Take time to heal before you dive back in the water. You want to swim without injury and with knowledge on what it takes to avoid the sharks.

The Dangers of Attraction

Now that you know you attract the types of men you think about most, what are you going to do to change your thinking? The dangerous part of attraction is that manipulative men are drawn to hurt and vulnerable women who seek some form of validation or significance; women who define themselves according to their relationships and what their man thinks about them. Manipulative men can sense women who are open game during a never-ending hunting season. They study women to better determine which ones to target. During its hunt if a lion spots two gazelles, one of which is noticeably injured, which one do you think is going to be targeted for consumption? Manipulators are those lions. Don't go out into the wild with your broken heart on your sleeve. A manipulative man sees that as an open invitation to pounce. He'll say all the right things and give you what you think you need at that moment, while running a masterful game that'll be detrimental for you in the end. In his mind he's the king of this jungle and you're nothing more than his next victim. Also, what you desire can't be obvious to onlookers. If it is, you're setting yourself up to attract manipulators who'll use that as the springboard that catapults them into your bed, bank account and whatever area they want 100% access to. As prey you'll become used to and comfortable with this type of man. You'll attract him more often than not and like an injured gazelle that, if given the choice, I'm sure it would rather be in a lion's presence than a lion's mouth. You'll keep manipulative men around as long as they doesn't eat you alive. Sad to say, but some women are comfortable with manipulative men so they tend to only attract those types. They dominate their thought process. They think all men alike anyway so why bother expecting anything different? They know the manipulator's game and intentions, and have become willing participants in their own manipulation. Their thinking? *"Why open up to someone new and risk being hurt anyway? Why not just stick with what I know?"* Women like this expect to experience hurt, but would rather deal with familiar than unfamiliar pain. The five reasons you just read may explain why you repeatedly attract the same types of men. You have to take the time to evolve and outgrow your box in order to meet great guys waiting for you outside of it. Unfortunately manipulative men are everywhere, but you can avoid them. You don't have to fall victim to their deceitful and hurtful ways. You can break free from this cycle by thinking and doing things differently. Don't let fear and pain be the obstacles that discourage you when it comes to dating, commitment and experiencing true love. Your pain shouldn't be taken lightly but you must overcome it so that you can experience healing, wholeness and happiness. Not all men are out to hurt you but many are; that's where being aware comes in handy. But don't become aware to a fault. Be cautious, but more importantly be willing to take a chance when you feel one is worth taking. Remember, with love comes certain risks but those risks have to be taken in order for you to achieve the type of love you desire. Changing certain things may seem risky but would you rather change your familiar ways when it comes to meeting men, dating and relationships, or would you rather continue with your normal patterns of behavior that lead to the same disappointing results?

Chapter Five – When the Dream Becomes a Nightmare

You're convinced the man you thought was "the one" is nothing more than a master manipulator. How could this be? What have you done? What do you do now? He has exposed his truth or his truth has been exposed. Either way, who he really is has finally come to the surface. Why did you not recognize all of this sooner? The answer? He skillfully pulled the wool over your eyes, blinding you to the reality of who he really is. He wanted to be the man you thought you needed, so he became him even though he never was him. He distracted you enough to cause you to ignore or not recognize red flags. He has mastered being a chameleon; he hid in plain sight. He was everything you thought you wanted until his true colors were revealed. This chapter will expose the chameleon, along with giving you three effective steps to take when the dream becomes a nightmare. Life is too short for continued victimization. You're better than him, and too good for him and men like him. Some men are professional liars and hiders, and they excel when it comes to covering up the truth and hiding who they really are. These types will make it hard for you to trust when it comes to opening up to the possibility of something new with someone new. In turn, that'll make it harder to build a healthy happy relationship.

Exposing the Chameleon

A *chameleon* is *a changeable, fickle, or inconstant person.*[6] How they appear one day will be totally different the next. Men who have mastered being a chameleon adapt and change according to the type of woman they're manipulating. Every woman may get a different version of him, while who he really is remains camouflaged. Most men have representatives they present to women in the beginning. They want to be chosen so they may send

---

[6] http://dictionary.reference.com/browse/chameleon

their representative to lay the ground work to ensure that happens. Chameleons are different; they change based on environment in order to gain access while hiding the true nature of their intentions. While other guys are vying for a woman's attention, a chameleon's goal is to gain entrance. Once inside he can really prey on a woman's hurt and vulnerabilities. With entrance comes control that makes it easier to manipulate feelings and create emotional attachments, making it harder for you to leave or forget about him. Chameleons are only concerned with the benefits that come from being involved with you. You're nothing more than a means to an end. They're tricky, and that's why you have to be careful. Watch your step and if you feel like they're hiding something, they are. Chameleons are good at that.

What to do When the Nightmare Sets In

1. Take Ownership

When the dream becomes a nightmare the first thing you need to do is take ownership of the access you gave and / or what you did to cause it. You're not responsible for his actions, but you are responsible for your decisions. Hold yourself accountable. It's the only way to truly move on after walking away. You have to own your part! Could it be you gave him entrance too soon? Too much access too fast? Did you give too much without getting anything in return? Did you give him a benefit of the doubt he didn't earn? You have to be honest with yourself. You have to be willing to take a hard look at yourself to see where you had a lapse in judgment. All of us have them, and the best thing you can do is recognize it, correct it and move on from it. Once you realize and accept where you went wrong, it'll be easier to break free from his hold.

2. <u>Implement a Firm No Return Policy</u>

You let him come back because you love him and he said he'd never hurt you again? Really? This monster damaged you almost beyond repair, yet you keep allowing him to come back. You keep sabotaging your healing and overall well-being to give a manipulator yet another chance to hurt you. Of course he's going to come back every time. Where else is he going to go? Who else does he have? If it's more beneficial to use you, why wouldn't he? Are you the only woman he's using? Probably not, but you get the point. The best relationships go through rough patches and sometimes a break up, however a healthy couple making up is different than you allowing a manipulator to play with your emotions to gain entrance back into your life. This man hurt you on purpose! He doesn't deserve another chance and you can't take that risk again. To hell with his apologies! Get rid of him and keep it moving. Forgive him when you're ready, but not for him, for you. Let go of any emotional attachments you have to him. When you choose to forgive, understand that you don't have to forget nor do you have to relive that pain. You don't owe him another chance. Keep in mind why you walked away. It'll be easier to stay away. His apologies are no guarantee that his manipulative and abusive behaviors won't continue. The only certainty you have that they won't is if you don't return. Cut off all communication and move on. No take backs!

3. <u>Get Over It! Get Over Him! Get A Life!</u>

You've been down. You may be down right now. But you're not out! Be determined! No matter what, he doesn't win! He doesn't break you! He won't have you crying, begging or caught up over him! You had a lapse in judgment and gave access to the wrong man, but that doesn't mean you can't make up for that mistake through healing, growth and change. In the end, YOU WIN! He thought he had you right where he wanted you; he thought you would give up and give in. Not this time! Accept no loss or defeat; accept no willingness to endure heartache after heartache. Don't let his actions cause you to question or doubt yourself, or give up on one day experiencing the love you desire and deserve. Take time to get over the pain and to especially get over him. Take control of your life back! Take control of your heart back! Yes it's easier said than done and he'll try to pull on your heartstrings to draw you back in, but you can't allow it! Don't you dare sit up and give up because a man got the best of you. You may feel damaged but you're not beyond repair. You're not damaged goods; stop telling yourself that. Shut down the pity parties and stop depressing yourself because you no longer feel like you deserve a good man. You do! The best thing you can do is learn from the experience and move forward. This is the perfect time to dine at that restaurant you've been wanting to try, or join that new health club in town. The perfect time to shop till you drop and enjoy your freedom. Treat yourself! Don't let him win! You may be hurt but you're not broken and you can overcome this. Do whatever it takes to let go and forget about him, and remember you. I know how it feels to be hurt by someone you loved and cared about once you realize they should've never been granted access in your life. I know how it feels when the dream becomes a nightmare. These are tough experiences to live through, but you have to. You have to get through them to become the best version of yourself and live your absolute best life as a gift to yourself!

Chapter Six – Overcoming Commitment Fears

It's hard to get back into the swing of things after an emotionally traumatic experience. The hurt is enough to make you want to hide from the world for a while. I encourage emotional sabbaticals but not to the extent where you seemingly drop of the face of the earth. Manipulative men are masters at breaking women down until they don't have the emotional strength or will to walk away from victimization, making it easier for them to be taken advantage of. After an investment of time, thoughts and feelings, the worst thing that can happen is for someone to purposely hurt you. Once a manipulator is exposed many women experience anger and frustration, before eventually shutting down completely. They swear to never commit to another man or relationship out of fear of the same dead end results. Building a loving and healthy relationship shouldn't be something you fear, but heartache can make you doubt the possibility. Manipulative men contribute to your commitment fears by causing you to believe that all men are like them. This is why they seek to damage you on purpose. When you view things from a place of hurt, you'll never see the beauty in who and what may be waiting for you on the other side. Precautionary measures have to be set in place to ensure that you steer clear of manipulators, but you can't become cautious to a fault, blocking the good because you fear the bad. You can't be afraid of moving on. You can't fear forward progress when you decide to get out there again. The following ten steps will help you get over your commitment fears and get on with your life. Implement them into your daily routine. Stop letting what a manipulator hold you up. You have a beautiful life ahead of you, so live like it!

Step One – Recognize the Difference

Don't fall into the trap of thinking that all men are the same. We're not. The hurt many women carry from one relationship to the next is a result of this stinking thinking. It's also why they continue to attract men who hurt them. Good men want you to trust them. They know it may take time, but they're willing to make the investment as long as you don't blame them for the pain another man caused. Most men are smart enough to know this is one of the main reasons a woman may not trust them, and why she chooses to remain emotionally distant and disconnected. Although your feelings are valid, you not trusting him is unfair. It may cost you the relationship. Yes he should earn your trust, but you have to be willing to let him. This is why I advocate for dating again after healing, not during what should be the healing process. Until you can give your all to another committed relationship, do your best to avoid one. You won't be happy with any man until you take time to heal, no matter how great he is. Good men do exist, and you deserve to be with one. Don't let stinking thinking rob you of that opportunity.

Step Two – Take Back Control!

Unknowingly a lot of women relinquish control of their emotions to men who claim to love them, only to end up manipulating them. When a manipulator knows he has the power to control a woman emotionally his goal will always be to keep her distracted and emotionally triggered. Saying all the right things and preying on exposed vulnerabilities all but guarantees who he really is will remain unnoticed until it's too late. When you finally realize who and what he is he'll have enough emotional control over you to keep you in a paralyzed state of unhappiness in a dysfunctional relationship. Take back control! Of your heart. Of your emotions. Of your time. It's time to get off of the emotional rollercoaster this man has you on and save yourself from future heartache. Make it a priority to disconnect from manipulators. If you don't they will continue to take advantage of you. Cut off all communication. All of it! You don't need him for anything, and there's nothing he needs you for that won't cause you more hurt. Close the door on all access he has to you, double lock it and destroy the key. IT'S OVER! If he burned you once, what do you think playing around his fire will do the next time? Once you get rid of him he'll try to pull on you emotionally. This is why cutting off all communication is really important. Don't give him even the slightest opportunity to manipulate how you feel. You control the outcome of this situation, and once you're done make up your mind to stay done! There's no need to be friends, associates or anything else that requires you to be cordial with this man. It's time to move on with your life.

Step Three – Don't be Afraid to be Alone

If you're used to being in a relationship you may become needy, thinking you need to be in a relationship in order to experience any level of happiness. Needing to always be with someone can open you up to attracting just about anybody, including manipulators more often than not. They can sense that neediness, and in some cases desperation. Coupled with the fear of abandonment and rejection, and a woman doesn't stand a chance when it comes to fighting off manipulative men who prey on her. The risk of being unhappy can't be greater than your desire to be experience true love. Unhealthy relationships are draining, and it's better to be full by yourself than empty with someone who doesn't deserve you. Without a man in their lives some women feel out of place, thinking that a relationship is proof that they have value. You have value without one. You're a queen without a king. You shine even if you're by yourself. Staying in a cycle of unhealthy relationships will cause damage no woman should have to endure; damage that will make it almost impossible to heal. No man validates you. You validate yourself! Alone time isn't a bad thing. You may feel lonely at times but that's better than experiencing everyday heartache in the presence of a manipulative man who will break you down as much as you allow him to. Being alone is perfect when you need time to and with yourself to heal, rebuild and get yourself all the way back together. Embrace alone time and use it as an opportunity to get to know you better, figure out what you really want, and build up enough emotional strength to never again relinquish control you should always have.

Step Four – Proper Judgment

Manipulative men can and will impair your judgment. That's the goal. In an impaired emotional and mental state you can only make unhealthy decisions. Once you take control back , keep your guards up and judge accordingly. I don't care what he says. I don't care what he does. I don't care how right for you he seems to be. Keep an emotionally and mentally safe distance to prevent impaired judgement. Make him prove himself to you. And if discomfort is present, understand it's there for a reason. Also, be mindful of familiar actions and behaviors that resemble that of manipulators from your past. If it walks like a duck, you know the rest. Stay focused on your emotional health and overall well-being. A manipulator will say anything to get his way; don't be fooled by words. Be patient. A man's true colors will always reveal who he really is.

Step Five – Love is Never Abusive

I want to take a few minutes to speak directly to women involved or previously involved in an abusive (physically, emotionally, and / or mentally) relationship. Any man who would abuse you doesn't love you. Read that again: Any man who would abuse you doesn't love you. There's no way he can love you and abuse you; the two don't coincide, they collide. Some will say *"Well that's just common sense"*, but millions of women are abused by men they think love them. For this reason among others they stay, hoping and praying for change. Fear also keeps a lot of women imprisoned in abusive relationships. It's not right to say *"Just leave"*, especially when we don't know why she can't or won't. One abusive experience should be more than enough for any woman to see that this is not the type of man she needs in her life, but circumstances make accepting this truth hard sometimes – especially when she genuinely loves him. No matter what a man is going through, he doesn't have the right to abuse you. It's not your fault and he has no right to blame you. He wants to take his anger and frustrations out on you because he's incapable of directing those emotions towards the sources that cause them. Plus, he sees you as the weaker vessel and wants to completely dominate you. With you he knows he can demonstrate a power and control he couldn't get away with anywhere else with anybody else. Millions of women have died from the abuse they endured because they were afraid to leave, couldn't leave, or actually believed the men abusing them loved them.

They started blaming themselves for the abuse, thinking that they did something to deserve it. An abusive man will never change. Even if you know examples of once abusive men who turned their lives around, you don't have time to take that chance on yours doing the same thing. Whatever you have to do to get away from him, do it! Whoever you need to contact to make sure he stays away from you, contact them! Whatever you have to do to protect yourself, do it! The potential of him changing doesn't and shouldn't trump who he is right now. Who you see right now is who he is, and you can't risk your life or overall well-being on the potential of things changing. If you find yourself only attracting abusive men, you really need to pinpoint those damaged areas in your life that draws them to you. Abusive men can sense brokenness and will pounce on you every chance they get. Work on you. Give yourself time. Change the way you think, and I promise the type of men you attract will change as well. You're not the problem, but you have the solution. You know the solution. You're the solution! Never take ownership of the blame an abusive man will try to place on you. You are not responsible for his abusive behaviors and it's not your fault. Abusers want to break their victims. Make them feel worthless. Even if you're at that point right now, please understand that your life has value and meaning, and you don't have to remain a victim. You're so much better and you deserve so much better. An abusive man will even tell you that no other man will ever want or love you because he's afraid that you'll one day realize that one actually will; a man that's one thousand times better than him. Never see yourself the way your abuser sees you! See yourself the way you were created to be seen, as a bright and beautiful woman who deserves a bright and beautiful life. An abusive experience cannot and should never be associated with love. Once love is associated with abuse you forfeit the opportunity of truly experiencing it until your thought process changes and you embrace healing over heartache.

Step Six – When the Pieces No Longer Fit, Don't Force It

After experiencing heartache don't talk yourself into staying in a relationship that's destined to fail. Walk away knowing that this wasn't the relationship for you. Couples who genuinely love each other may experience periods of separation as they work through certain issues that affect the growth of their relationship. That's not the same as convincing yourself that staying with an manipulative man is actually a good idea. It's not! Stop giving him the benefit of the doubt. Stop choosing him over yourself. This relationship won't work. It can't work. And that's a blessing. Master manipulators are good at leaving behind enough emotional, mental or physical traces of themselves to prey on your emotions when you start missing them or find yourself feeling lonely. After you cut them off they will do whatever it takes to see just how far you're willing to let them go before you let them come back. They don't miss or need you, but they do miss and need the benefits of being involved with you. Don't let a manipulative man force his way back into your life. Change your number if you have to. Move if you need to. Yes these may seem like drastic measures but you need to do whatever is required to detox from his toxicity. Remember the bad times. Remember how he made you feel. Remember why you closed off all access he had to you. Throw away anything he left at your place. If he needed it that bad he would've taken it with him. You don't need to meet up to give it to him. You don't need to drop it off and he doesn't need to pick it up. Don't let him play you again. Can things change? Sure. Will he change? Probably not. Has he changed? No. You don't need him in your life. He doesn't fit in your life, so don't force something that isn't and shouldn't be there. This type of man is a genius when it comes to making a woman believe he fits in their life. He'll say and do anything to persuade and trick you into going against your better judgment. If he can convince you that you need him, you'll be the one doing whatever it takes to keep him. That makes it so much easier for him to manipulate you. You have to rid yourself of every trace of him so you can move on. This is about you and your life! Kick him out and keep him out.

Step Seven – Be on Guard but Approachable

After heartache, it's hard for some women to trust men again. Every man is deemed untrustworthy until he earns trust. This is a good way to be, but it can also be very stifling if taken to the extreme. Not every man is out to hurt you, and while you should vet every potential partner, you need to understand that what an old man did in the past is no reflection of what a new man will do in the present and future. Good or bad. I get that you're protecting yourself and you should, but leave just enough emotional breathing room to be able to feel when someone and something is right for you. When you're ready to get back out there, be on guard but also approachable. Master engaging in conversation without granting access. If he's someone you want to get to know you're going to have to converse with him, but that doesn't mean you have to expose or even share certain vulnerabilities until you fully trust him. A man who feels you're worth the investment will understand why you're on guard. He'll have no problem demonstrating patience with you, and he'll put forth the effort it takes to help you trust him. Remain on guard though. He might be saying and doing all the right things, but that doesn't mean he's the right guy for you. The feeling out process takes time; give yourself all the time you need. Manipulators have mastered keeping up appearances for prolonged periods of time so you have to feel every man out. Wait for their true colors to show; they will because they always do. Be proactive in your defense. Protect your heart from the beginning. Reactive responses happen after you're blindsided, and by then it's too late. Take as much time as you need to heal, and once you're ready to get back into the dating game be on guard but also know when to let someone in.

Step Eight – Fear is Not More Important than Happiness

Fear doesn't keep you safe it keeps you imprisoned. It keeps you estranged from happiness and constantly approaching every dating or potential relationship experience with a heightened level of unhealthy anxiety. Certain risks are involved when it comes to any new experience. Fear doesn't eliminate those risks, it eliminates you being able to embrace the happiness that may come as a result of you taking a chance. You still desire to love and be loved, and it's going to take a leap of faith on your part to do both. You have to make the decision on which one you'd rather live with. Fear or happiness? I understand that getting close to someone new is scary, but how will you know unless you go for it? When you trust him and feel comfortable enough to grant access, you have to be willing to take the risk to reap the reward. If fear is your crutch, you will limp into every relationship emotionally wounded and incapable of embracing happiness because fear will always be in the place where the happiness you desire belongs.

Step Nine – Find Your Healing Place

Unresolved hurt will cause you to exist in a state of misery and sadness, thinking that things will never go right for you so you might as well give up on love. A lot of women don't take enough time to heal and get to know themselves again before lunging into another destructive relationship. Hurt will keep you making dangerous moves like this, and that's why healing is imperative. There is no set time frame. Take as much time as you need, but make healing a priority. Do whatever works for you to move yourself from pain to promise. Ignoring the hurt won't make it go away, it'll actually make things worse and cause you to attract men who are only capable of hurting you. After heartbreak you have to come to a place in your life where you are willing to heal completely before trying again, and you're unwilling to allow your relationship decisions to be made from a place of pain. The success of your best relationship depends on your willingness to heal and get over the most painful one(s).

Step Ten – Commitment is an Opportunity

It's imperative that you overcome the fear of rejection and abandonment, and master connecting with men without becoming emotionally attached to them. This takes time but it's definitely possible and a reasonable expectation you should have of yourself. It liberates you from the past trauma that continues to haunt you and sabotage your relationships. Heal first. Give yourself time. Afterwards, see commitment as an opportunity, a new endeavor that will contribute to the happiness you already have once a man proves he's worth it. Commitment is powerful when it's put into action. That's why who you choose to commit to must be worth it or you'll just experience another imitation of it. Not every man is the same, but the man who truly wants to be with you must earn his place in your life. Once he does, don't let what others have done ruin the possibility. These ten steps won't be easy to master. It takes time for them to become habits, results aren't automatic in every case but in most cases, and a tendency to revert back to your old ways will always creep up on you when you least expect it. Don't let your happiness be deterred by past failures and heartbreak. Fear will hold you hostage in that place of pain for as long as you allow. You have the power to take your life back! You have the power to maintain emotional clarity and stability. The only person who can stop you from breaking through is you. That may read cliché, but it's the truth. I declare you will see wonderful changes take place in your life. You'll no longer fear moving on. And once you heal, don't give another man the power to hurt you, but give a man who's worth it the opportunity to love you.

Chapter Seven – Numbers Don't Lie

No matter what you do or how hard you try, some people will never change. Think about it this way: 2 + 2 will never equal 5. No matter what you do. No matter how you rearrange the numbers. The fact remains that the answer will never be 5, even if you want it to be. This is how you should view manipulative men. Even if they say they're changing or have changed, the risk is far too great to take a chance on someone who has already proven themselves to be toxic. There's a small chance they have changed, but the odds are more in favor of them just saying they have to get you back so they can eventually hurt you again. Don't fall for it! Why do we try to change unchangeable people? Why do we attempt to save someone who doesn't want to be saved from themselves, when we really need to save ourselves from them? Because we love them? Because we want to see them do better? Both are good points to consider, but not good enough reasons to stay. When the situation is toxic why do we still try to manipulate the circumstances just enough so that the obvious won't be so obvious? For example, a woman is involved with a manipulative man. Even though she's experienced his toxic behaviors, she still tries to convince herself (and others) that he's not the way he really is. For her to accept the truth she first has to accept that she's been duped by the lie. A lot of people think they're too smart to be manipulated, but none of us are. That's why we have to stand on guard when it comes to who we grant access to. Admitting and accepting that you've been played is hard, and denial seems to add a bit of comfort during the emotional turbulence. I have counseled women and men who prefer living in denial instead of accepting the truth for what it is. No matter how you try to rearrange the numbers, two plus two will always equal four; the same goes for manipulative men. No matter how great you want them to seem to yourself and others, the fact remains that they're manipulators. An abusive relationship is an abusive relationship, whether you are emotionally, verbally and / or physically abused once or multiple times. Stop trying to change the facts in hopes that who you're dealing with and what you're going through is somehow different than what it really is. The hurt and disappointment is written all over your face, yet you're still in denial? Why? The situation, involvement or relationship is toxic and dysfunctional. You need to do what's best for you and let it go. End the cycle or remain a victim of it.

Who are you to rescue him anyway?

Wonder Woman was a 1970s heroine with super powers and abilities, who flew around in an invisible jet catching criminals with her golden lasso. This isn't you, and he's no victim in need of rescue. Any man expecting you to be his savior is foolish and doesn't deserve you. You have to get sick and tired of the lies, apologies, manipulation and deception because he can't get it together. You have to get sick and tired of him wasting your time and frowning on your efforts when it comes to your relationship. You have to realize that you can't save him from himself, especially if he thinks he's okay the way he is. It's not your responsibility to be his saving grace. His salvation isn't your burden to bear. I get that relationships aren't always easy, but when it comes to rescuing someone from themselves you need to wake up and see the light. You need to understand that's not your job. You're not responsible for his rescue nor obligated to lead him to it. You trying to save him all but guarantees you lose yourself in the process. Once you accept that a manipulative man is this way by choice, nothing more needs to be said or done. It'll be easier to let go and move on. Don't waste your time hoping for a change that may never come. Don't waste your time playing the odds. Numbers don't lie, and if you're gambling with your heart more than likely you're going to lose.

It's Simple Arithmetic

Arithmetic is the most elementary branch of mathematics. When used to delineate a manipulative man's behaviors, arithmetic can mean *"the method of processing data with information, evidence and facts."* You have to take your time and process everything that's in front of you when it comes to the man you're involved with. Let's take a closer look at how arithmetic can be used to process data when it comes to discovering whether or not your man is a manipulator.

Information

Information is *knowledge communicated or received concerning a particular fact or circumstance; news.*[7] Pretty simple right? The information may or may not be factual, so you have to make sure it's received and processed carefully. For example, various sources could inform

---

[7] http://dictionary.reference.com/browse/information

you that your man is up to no good. These sources could be friends, family members or other people who know the two of you are together. How do you take it? What reasons do you have to trust them? What reasons do you have not to trust them? Why would they lie? Something inside of you is telling you to believe them, but what if they're wrong? Then what? You don't want to just confront him with accusations. You don't want to believe the worst about your man, but you also want to believe that certain people are genuinely looking out for you when they tell you certain things. The best way to process this information is to take what's said and contemplate how it applies to his behaviors. Pay closer attention to his actions and his non-verbal communication. Does he spend more time out than with you? Based on how you feel and what you already know, is there a chance he's hiding someone or something from you? Have you been ignoring red flags that basically confirm what you've been told? The signs may be there, but they're not always easily detected. Most manipulators are experts when it comes to covering their tracks, and that's why it's always best to watch their actions and compare the amount of recreational time they spend with you to the amount of recreational time they spend without you. You don't want to come across suspicious and the worst thing you can do is confront a suspected manipulator with inaccurate or assumed information. This is why you have to carefully process what you've been told before confronting him. In the end, if the information turns out to be true you can be thankful that you have people in your life who care enough about your well-being to tell you the truth. If it turns out to be false, be thankful that you were wise enough not to let people dictate the outcome of your relationship.

Evidence

Evidence is *something that makes plain or clear; an indication or sign.*[8] After information is received part of processing carefully requires having evidence that proves the information to be true or false. The type of evidence can vary but the end result is it should help determine your next step. Collecting evidence can be the difficult part, especially when it comes to master manipulators because they cover their tracks very well. But even the most masterful slip up every now and then. Trust your gut. If you feel something is off, something is off! That feeling should be more than enough for you to know what you need to do next, but I understand some of us need something we can actually see to go along with how we feel. Text messages, emails, private phone calls and other suspicious behaviors can provide a gold mine of evidence, but retrieving the information you need won't be easy and I'll never advocate for violating

---

[8] http://dictionary.reference.com/browse/evidence

anyone's privacy. So ask. Out of the blue. By surprise. Without warning. Ask can you see his phone and read his text messages and / or emails. He may ask you why, and to that question you respond because you have some concerns. That's it. He'll question you about what kind of concerns, but at this point that information doesn't need to be relayed. If he goes off or gets immediately defensive, you already know what that means. If he starts asking you questions in an attempt to distract you from what it is that you're requesting, you already know what that means. Yes we're all entitled to privacy but sometimes certain accommodations should be made if it helps our partners feel better about being involved with us. Requesting this information means you won't be violating his privacy and you'll be able to see how he responds to your request, and that should help tremendously when it comes to what steps you need to take next. He'll ask if you trust him or not and may even try to make you feel bad about requesting certain access.

Don't waiver. Stand firm on needing to see and also be willing to show. This may seem childish or like you're "doing too much", but when it comes to matters of the heart you have to avoid getting hurt the best way you can. Plus, you don't want to falsely accuse him, and once the access is granted and you see what you need to see, you can explain to him why you made the request in the first place. Because of these actions he may begin to think you have trust issues, and that's okay. If he really wants to be with you he'll understand why you did what you felt you needed to do. Plus, if he's innocent he'll appreciate you not just jumping to conclusions based on what you were told by others. I know you don't want to seem like the insecure or jealous type, but you have to think about your overall well-being. If there are signs you may be at risk of being manipulated you have to look into why those signs exist. That, or you could end the relationship and keep it moving if it's not worth all the trouble. The choice is yours, as it should be. Is making this request an absolutely certain way to get the evidence you need? No, but no method is. Unless he confesses his wrongdoings to you, finding out about them is going to take some work or divine intervention. Approach him with your requests in a calm manner, even if you're requesting access to something I didn't list. You may want to know his whereabouts on a certain day, or who a certain woman is that he's been seen with. Be clear with what you want and stand firm. Expect honesty. In most cases, when a man is being questioned in a certain way or when certain requests are being made he already knows you know something. It's up to him to be forthcoming or evasive. One reaction or the other will help prove his innocence or guilt. To be clear, I am in no way advocating for privacy violations. Request to see what you want and need to know. If you feel the concerns or suspicions you have are warranted, ask him. Make the request. I am a firm believer in privacy and personal space, but if you can avoid being blindsided by manipulation and heartache you have to do whatever it takes to ensure that you don't emotionally crash and burn. He's going to say, *"You should just trust me"*, and you should but obviously you don't fully trust him for a reason. Maybe it's you, maybe it's him, but the reason is more than enough. Would it be better to just end things? In my opinion, yes. Why be with someone you don't fully trust? What else are you trying to see or figure out? But then again you have people who hate seeing the two of you together so they may make up something to plant seeds of doubt in your mind. If you feel the relationship is worth holding on to at least until you figure everything out, then by all means stay. If the involvement is new then you might just want to call it a wash and move on. I don't recommend these steps unless you're involved with someone on what you consider to be a level of serious commitment. Be transparent and expect transparency. Some of what I'm sharing may seem a bit extreme, but would you rather be a bit extreme and glad you know the truth or continue not knowing and end up heartbroken all over again? Just an FYI - Most manipulating men hide suspicious text messages and photos, and many have more than one email account; master manipulators may even have more than one phone number even though they only have one phone; a lot of them have more than one though. There are various smartphone apps that make all of this possible. Research them and if you see these apps installed on his phone you already know what it is. Don't feel bad for wanting to know the truth, and don't let him make you feel bad. If the truth sets you free, then it's the truth that will help you move forward. Manipulative men will never tell you they're manipulating you. Put him on notice anyway if you feel the need to. He'll know why.

Facts

Facts are *things that actually exist; reality; truth.*[9] Be sure you can handle the truth before you seek it. If you're

---

[9] http://dictionary.reference.com/browse/facts

just going to deny the truth that you find, don't waste your time. Be ready to make moves if the truth reveals heartbreak is on the horizon. Facts are a result of evidence. Facts are the *"It is what it is"* part of the process. He's either innocent or guilty. Facts will determine this for you. Facts will reveal the manipulative ways you've turned a blind eye. Facts will sound the alarm you've been ignoring unintentionally. Facts will make red flags shine even brighter. Once you have facts in hand, what more needs to be said or done? If the relationship doesn't mean that much to you and too many doubts about him have already surfaced, let it go without going through all the extra. However, if you've developed an emotional bond with this man and you're not 100% sure what's being said about him is true or why you're feeling a certain way, seek the truth for yourself. Manipulative men seem sincere, but that doesn't mean they care. If they did they wouldn't be manipulators. You may never know you're with a man who genuinely doesn't care about you, so you have to make sure you care about yourself at all times. When the facts prove he's a manipulator let him go immediately! When the facts prove he's insensitive and abusive, let him go. No matter how much it hurts, you have to let him go. You can't change him and you shouldn't try! You have to deal with the pain now, but be happy you chose to do so voluntarily instead of waiting until you're forced to do so when he hurts you for the last time. When involved and emotionally attached to a manipulative man, you have to understand that disappointment is coming. Be the one to welcome it now so your healing process can be made easier instead of waiting until heartbreak hits you out of nowhere, making your healing process that much harder and longer. The *arithmetic* of it all is easy to understand, you just have to be willing to learn and master proper computing. Yes it's sad that these extreme measures even have to be taken, but when you're involved with someone who refuses to be 100% honest about who they are and their intentions you have to do whatever needs to be done. The truth won't always come easy, sometimes you have to go on the hunt for it. Though it may hurt when you find it, you'll feel so much better once you know. No matter how hard you try, until he decides to change a manipulative man will always be a manipulative man. Nothing you do will ever change that! No matter what, two plus two will always equal four. Always.

Chapter Eight – Does He Really Understand?

Manipulative men have studied women to better understand and know how to relate and respond to them. This makes the task of manipulating them much easier. When a man's primary goal is to manipulate a woman he takes as much time as he assumes he needs to gain enough insight on her to better position himself for success. When a man targets a specific woman he puts her in one of three categories.

1. **Easy** – This woman will be easy to manipulate. It won't take much time or effort because she's already displayed certain weaknesses and vulnerabilities that are basically doing the job for him.

2. **A Challenge** – This woman has her guards up. She's been through some things but she's still hopeful. It's going to take some time and

effort but she'll definitely open up as long as he keeps saying and doing what she considers are the right things.

3. <u>**Almost Impossible**</u> – This woman will be a hard to fool. She's guarded, emotionally unavailable and has lost all hope as it relates to meeting a man who isn't full of it. She can spot BS from a mile away and she's not into wasting her time. Unless he's up for the challenge, this is the type of women a manipulative man will steer clear of. In his mind it will take too long to break her, and he's not into investing that kind of time when there are so many other women he can have quicker success with.

Once a manipulative man determines what type of woman you are, how he interacts with you will be determined by which category he places you in. He'll relate to you to get to you, and the more open you are the better his chances. He knows this so he'll use understanding to open you up and gain access that you otherwise wouldn't give him, especially not as soon as he wants you to. You have to know that just because a man seems to understand you it doesn't mean he does authentic. When it comes to manipulative men, it means they're good at what they do. Pretending to understand and actually understanding are two completely different things. As you now know, manipulating men feed off of information, so the more you give the better his chances are of manipulating you. Think about everything you've told him so far. Is it that he really understands you or is he just going off of what you've said and feeding it back to you in a different way?

Is it Real or Not?

Knowing the difference between understanding and pseudo-understanding is key. An understanding man is an investing man (as outlined in chapter two), and he will take time to learn about you, not only based on the information you share but also based on spending time with you and getting to know you. He can relate based on his own life experiences, and he never presses you for information that could potentially damage you. He's patient, and he prefers that things flow smoothly rather than quickly. Pseudo-understanding is the appearance of understanding; an illusion. It's when a man takes the information you gave him and twists it to fit whatever narrative he's trying to present to make you feel like he actually understands you. Initially, your comfort is priority. It's the only way he can get you to trust him enough to let your guards down. Instead of letting things flow naturally he'll ask probing questions, especially when it comes to your feelings, and pretend to listen with intent and personal interest because he wants you to trust him. Plus, this way he comes across sensitive and kind, as if he really cares about you. What happens when you expose a weakness to a predator? You get pounced on. When you expose certain weaknesses to a manipulative man, he uses those moments of vulnerability to pounce on you when your guard's down. This is how he sets his trap. How do you feel when a man tells you the type of woman "he thinks" you are? Do you feel understood? Recognized? Does it somehow validate how you've been feeling? It's easy for a man to tell you what kind of woman you are after you've already told him. He'll tell you something like *"You're a woman who desires to be loved and cared for, and not hurt again like you've been in the past. I get it."* after you tell him *"I've been hurt, and I just don't want to go through that kind of heartache again."* You're making it just that easy for him. He'll tell you something like *"I know you're afraid of being hurt again, and I promise I'l never hurt you."* after you tell him *"I'm scared of getting too close to someone because of what I've gone through in the past."* As you can see, it's a continual regurgitation of information when it comes to him convincing you that he understands. You're giving him the arsenal he needs to wage emotional war against you. He's using the information you're giving him to tear down your defenses, and the end result will be him causing you a major amount of damage and heartache. If you feel a man is investing time into truly understanding you, feel free to give him access when the time is right. However, if you notice that a man is being repetitive when it comes to his conversations with you, beware and don't take lightly the fact that he may be trying to manipulate you. Keep your guards up until you feel totally and completely safe. It's up to you to protect yourself. You're not looking to waste time dealing with imposters or impressers right? You want an investor. You desire a man who's going to contribute to your happiness, not destroy it. Most manipulative men overcompensate when it comes to information regurgitation. They have a tendency of giving way too much information back to you in hopes of you giving them that *"WOW!"* effect during the conversation. You saying *"Wow, you really do understand me"*, let's a manipulative man know that you're ready to be pounced on. He knows he has you right where he wants you. When he starts giving back too much of what you already gave to him, be cautious. Until you're 100% sure that he's genuine, develop no emotional attachments and grant no access. A man who understands you is inquisitive and interested more in how the two of you relate to each other. He shows interest by sharing his thoughts and feelings with you, not expecting it to be you just sharing yours with him. Manipulative men share very little about themselves and, instead of being inquisitive and seeking to sincerely understand you, they take what information you give to them and give it back to you in a manner that's seemingly different but actually the same. There's nothing wrong with a man wanting to genuinely understand you, just make sure when he's attempting to do so he's actually trying to understand you and not pretending to because of manipulative intentions.

Chapter Nine – It's Chess, Not Checkers

Chess is a game of thought, skill and strategy. A master chess player outplays their opponent by utilizing effective preemptive strategies. There are master manipulators who approach women with preemptive strikes to ensure they win the game. The attacks are subtle yet skillful enough to cause a break in a woman's defenses without her even knowing it. To help you defeat manipulative grandmasters I am going to give you three techniques to use when you feel like you've been approached by a manipulator. I'm using chess references to paint a clearer picture as to how manipulators move and how you can strategically eliminate the possibility of falling victim to their advances.

What's Your Strategy?

One of the most important strategies to master when playing against a formidable opponent is to think several moves ahead of them. A grandmaster not only concentrates on their moves but on the moves of their opponent as well; they think beyond the moment. Chess is a game that requires patience and concentration. These are two attributes you should master in your relationships. In order for you to think moves ahead of him you have to strategically plan yours and predict his. That may take some time. You can't rush the process; you have to think beyond the surface, beyond what he's telling you, and concentrate more on what he's showing you – what his actions are revealing to you. Concentrate on how you feel and what your gut is telling you about him. Even if you've just met him, your instincts will kick in immediately and begin to tell you almost everything you need to know. Don't drown out that inner voice because he may look good or what he's saying may sound good. If you feel he's worth your time then take your time and feel him out as you strategize your next move and predict his.

Game of Wit

To outwit an opponent you must first understand
what they understand, and comprehend things from
their purview; try to see what they see. You also have
to be willing to accept that this man may be a
manipulator. Don't go through all of the trouble if
you're just going to deny that he is who and what he
is. He may not be manipulative, but then again he
just might. The best way to find out is to put
yourself in his position. Figure out what it is that he
wants from you so you can already be ready when he
makes his move. Also, before you get attached to
any man it's best that you understand the concept of
outwit over dimwit. A dimwitted person is someone
who's stupid or does something out of stupidity. To
go into a new dating experience and open yourself
up to a new relationship without first understanding
what a man's agenda is, is quite dimwitted. You're
setting yourself up to be hurt if you don't have a
strategy that helps you figure out his intentions; or if

you ignore the results of your strategy and give him the benefit of the doubt anyway just because you like him. "Like" will lead to heartache if you're not careful. You have to be smart. You have to use intelligence when dealing with a man you have certain RESERVATIONS about. Study his play and master his moves. Question if you're ready for the moves that he's attempting to make, question his motives behind certain conversations, and see yourself the way your gut is telling you he sees you. You may not like it, but at least you'll know. That voice in your head may be telling you something that you don't want to hear, but it could be that one thing that saves you from a world of hurt. When you strategize and begin to see yourself the way he sees you, you may find out that he genuinely likes you. However, you may find out that he has a specific plan in mind when it comes to you; one that's not in your best interest. Be smart and on guard when interacting with him so you don't become dimwitted with your moves. Develop your strategy, trust your gut and listen to what that voice is telling you. You can't go wrong when you plan ahead, trust and listen.

<u>WIN!</u>

The main objective of chess is not how many of your opponent's pieces you can take but the moves you can make that will stop them. You're opponent can have minimal pieces left on the board and still win if you're not careful. Chess involves everything you should master before venturing into something new with someone new. You must have a strategy, understanding, insight and patience in order to move throughout the game successfully. You must remain moves ahead of your opponent in order to figure out their motive. When it comes to dating you must be willing to remain emotionally detached until you know beyond any doubt that an emotional attachment won't end up detrimental for you. Be mindful and cautious when it comes to your involvements because not every man you meet is honest and sincere. Most aren't. If you don't look out for you, who will? Who will protect you from heartache? You win when he concedes and leaves or when the truth is the only move he has left. This is when you have accomplished a successful checkmate.

Chapter Ten – Simple vs. Simple-Minded

In aggregate, men aren't complicated beings. Most of us are simple, but that doesn't mean we're simple-minded. Whatever we take the time to study we tend to master, including manipulating women. Too many women assume that most men are incapable of seeing beyond the surface and using emotional intellect to connect with them. They think we're driven by sex or sexual desires, and therefore that makes us and our intentions easy to figure out. While this may be true for some men, please understand that master manipulators have developed a skill set they use to target and manipulate specific types of women. They know how to play the game. They know all the right words to say and all the right things to do. They already know what you think they're after so their main goal is to get you to think otherwise even if you're right. You may be of superior intellect but that doesn't mean you can't be duped. By definition, **simple** means *something or* *someone that is easy to understand, not complex or compound; not complicated.*[10] This is most men. It doesn't mean that we're intellectually or emotionally inferior, it just means that we're more black and white than gray. We're more "it is what it is" than wondering what it could be. By definition, **simple-minded** is *a person whose mental capacities or capabilities are free of deceit or guile; artless or unsophisticated, lacking in mental acuteness or sense; mentally deficient.*[11] Don't fool yourself into thinking that most men are simple-minded. We're not, and when you're dealing with a master manipulator please understand that he has perfected his craft and therefore his prowess shouldn't be taken lightly. It doesn't take much to figure out most men. I say most because the manipulative ones are masters of disguise so it may take a little more effort to figure them out. Most men share like attributes when it comes to communicating, responding, reacting and dealing with certain relationship issues.

---

[10] http://dictionary.reference.com/browse/simple

[11] http://dictionary.reference.com/browse/simple-minded

Just because a man is simple doesn't mean he's clueless. In most cases he already knows exactly what it'll take to win you over. Coupling that knowledge with manipulative intentions, and even the simplest of men can be very dangerous. While you may be dissecting and overthinking every phase of your involvement with a man, he's making simple yet strategic moves to get to his desired result, whether it's good or bad. You taking the more complex route doesn't automatically mean you'll avoid his trap if he's a manipulator. Of course the initial encounter will speak volumes as it relates to what he's really after. Going back to that gut feeling and voice in your head, from his initial approach you'll know if he's a go or no if you pay attention. You'll know whether or not to share a drink with him, exchange numbers with him, leave with him, or even if you'll eventually be intimate with him. You'll get certain vibes that if paid attention to will help guide your decision making. A seasoned manipulator is a master of the game, so you have to tread lightly when you feel like he's setting you up to be played. He's an expert at playing the role and getting you to wrestle with and go against your better judgment. He'll play into you being intellectually superior and more complex emotionally just to get you to overthink and pay no attention to the simple route he's taking you on. Overthinking tends to cloud judgement, and that's exactly what he wants. Don't play battle of the brains with manipulators. Someone has to lose, and most of the time it's the woman who does. One of the most common ways a man manipulates a woman is him leading her to believe he lacks the smarts to trick her; that's the trick. It's when she thinks she has the mental upper hand that he goes in for the emotional kill.

Chapter Eleven – Letting Go of Trust Issues & Abandonment Fears

Trust issues make it hard to begin something new with someone new for understandable reasons. No one wants to be hurt, and after you experience it you do all you can to prevent it. Every man gets the same treatment. Even the good guys are deemed untrustworthy, even though they weren't the ones who hurt you. Their presence reminds you of the risks you've already taken that didn't work out. Because of this, they don't get the benefit of the doubt or the opportunity to get to know you. This is how it should be when it comes to the bad guys, but you miss out on the potential of something great when you put good guys in the same category. On top of trust issues, you may be dealing with abandonment fears as well. These fears affect all of your relationships, not just the ones you have with men. These fears may stem from your childhood. You may feel like everyone will leave at some point.

Every time you try to get close to someone you begin to fear that no matter how much you love them they'll eventually leave you. This fear forces you to keep everyone at an emotionally safe distance. Your issues with trust and abandonment make it impossible for you to open up to someone new. You believe every man is out to hurt and manipulate you. You run from love because of the pain you associate with it. You nurse your trust issues and abandonment fears and never effectively deal with them because it's easier to accept the problem as reality than to figure out a solution that works in your favor. You're insecure when it comes to dating, relationships and love. You think you're not good enough, as if you don't deserve a good man. You can't seem to let go and move forward because you're constantly reminding yourself that no man is to be trusted and no love is permanent. You doubt yourself. You doubt others. You have every right to feel this way, but how long will you allow yourself to be held captive by what has happened to you?

What's sad and ironic is what you fear most will always happen because it's that fear that continually causes you to attract manipulators. This is why every time you decide to give it one more try you always attract the guy you've been trying to keep away. Until you deal with your trust issues and abandonment fears and heal from them they'll always be the catalyst that sets you up to be played. Manipulative men are drawn to emotional injury and weakness, to wounds that haven't been given the aid needed to heal. They're vultures, and the only way to get rid of vultures is to show signs of life. You show signs of life by healing, finding your true self again and moving forward. Of course you should always proceed with caution, but you need to develop a confidence that puts manipulators on notice! A confidence that lets it be known that you are not to be played with. No matter what happened or what may be happening, love yourself way too much to wallow in misery. Love yourself way too much to allow pain to dictate how you trust. Love yourself way too much to feel unworthy and undeserving. Develop an inner-security that defeats any self-doubt or self-hatred you have. In order for you to heal and let go of trust issues and abandonment fears you need to empower yourself to be happy with you. It takes you believing in you and not worrying about what others have done, are doing or will try to do. Inner-security takes the distortion away so you can see clearly who and what's in front of you, and who and what to give access to. You're responsible for your healing and overall well-being, and you have to invest the time to make the process work. Start today on the path of self-rediscovery and inner-security. No matter what others have said or done; no matter who comes or who goes. Shout *"NO MORE!"* to heartache, abuse, misery and insecurity. This is your day to celebrate your victory over trust issues and abandonment fears that cause you to keep yourself away from some of the best things that have the potential of happening in your life. Be wise in your decision making and be anxious for nothing.

Don't let worry derail you, and take your time when it comes to dating, relationships and love. Forgive those who have hurt you. Forgive those who have abandoned you. Set them free from the imprisonment of your unforgiveness so you can be set free from the imprisonment of their offense. Change your mind about who you are and understand that you're worthy and deserving. Change your mind about men in general, and don't let yourself hate all men because of your experiences with some men. That hatred will only make you bitter. Be cautious but confident, aware of the men you give access to and unaccepting of anything less than what you know you deserve. Believe in yourself and let no one define or validate you. You define and validate yourself! Change your heart and your mind in order to experience complete healing and emotional recovery.

Conclusion – Men Are Not Your Enemy

I hope this book has equipped you with enough insight and understanding to see, know and overcome manipulation. This was not a man-hating book. The primary purpose of this book was to expose manipulators! To detail the actions of men who prey on emotionally wounded and vulnerable women. Men whose only intention is to deceive, use, abuse and hurt women. Men are not your enemy. Manipulators are. No man is perfect but good men do exist. Manipulators are the ones you must protect yourself from. The monsters who care nothing about you. The emotionally, mentally, verbally and / or physically abusive men who hurt women because they refuse to deal with their issues and confront their demons. Don't feel sorry for them. Don't give them the benefit of the doubt. Don't try to change them. Apply the information in this book to your everyday life and stay away from them! Don't feed or give into their ego or narcissism, and never give them the power to make you feel less than. It's not your job to save them from themselves. They'll learn the hard way that you can't go through life hurting people and expect everything to work in your favor. Let them carry the burden of their brokenness and insecurity, That's not your responsibility.

Manipulators are emotional terrorists who will stop at nothing when it comes to destroying everything you love about yourself, because it's when you're at your lowest that they can take full advantage without any real resistance. I wrote this book to give you a knowledgeable tool you can use to protect yourself from manipulators. A knowledgeable tool that helps you quickly recognize the signs of manipulation. The information, steps, tips and techniques you read about will help you uncover manipulation, expose emotional terrorists and rediscover yourself. You read this book, so that means you're open to change. I'm proud of you. Now apply it! Who you attract and how you interact with men won't change without your effort. Application is key. More than likely you won't remember everything. You may have to read this book again. You may have another lapse in judgment. That's okay. Keep applying what you learn until you do and choose better; until it becomes second nature. One thing you can't do is turn back the hands of time. Stop dwelling on your past. It's over! Let it go. Stressing over it is not going to change it, and constantly looking back makes it impossible to move forward. I know it's easier said than done, but you owe it to yourself to let it go. The onus is on you. You are responsible for your healing and overall well-being. It's your time to shine. Embrace it. No one and nothing can do the work for you. No author, coach, mentor or expert can do the work for you. They can help you along the way, but ultimately it's all on you to uncover and rediscover. Uncover what you need to change and where you need to heal, and rediscover the phenomenal woman you are. Make being an overcomer a daily habit. No matter who. No matter what. You overcome! Unpack your emotional baggage, sort it out and work it out. You got this! You are worthy and deserving of all things beautiful when it comes to life, dating, relationships, love and happiness. A happiness that you discover within and for yourself. A happiness that you'll only allow the right man to contribute to.

What's Next?

In this space I want you to write down what's next for you on your journey to overcoming, tear out the pages and hang them in a location where you can see and read them every day. This will be your daily reminder of the happiness ahead and the decrees you need to make over and manifest in your life.